Black Royals:
Queen Charlotte

Joysetta Marsh Pearse

Illustrator

Fatimah T. White

DEDICATION

To Julius Otto Pearse, who introduced me to serious study of African American history, and to the memory of the late James Rose, Ph.D., co-author of Black Genesis, who became our mentor for genealogical studies.

CONTENTS

ACKNOWLEDGMENTS

Special thanks to Minna Dunn, Art Director and Curator at the African American Museum of Nassau County who took our Queen Charlotte exhibit on a promotional tour to Toronto, Canada; Rochester, New York; Martha's Vineyard, Massachusetts; Newport, Rhode Island; and Washington, DC. She returned with a list of exhibit viewers who implored us to produce literature to accompany the exhibit, and to make it available to them. This mini-book is the result.

1 THE QUEEN

Figure 1 Queen Charlotte

Sophia Charlotte of Mecklenburg- Strelitz was born 19 May 1744, in Mirow, Duchy of Mecklenburg-Strelitz, Germany. She was the daughter of Charles, Prince of Mirow and Elisabeth Albertine, who was the Duchess of Saxe-Hildburghausen. At the age of seventeen, on 8 September 1761, Charlotte married King George III at Saint James Palace, in London. She had just arrived on the shore of her new home the day before, having had no prior meeting with the king or any members of the royal family. She spoke no English, on arrival, but is said to have quickly learned to speak the language, albeit, with a heavy German accent. She was fluent in French, and read some Latin.

Most Americans are familiar with George III, as he was sovereign at the time the Continental Congress sent him the Declaration of Independence.

Figure 2 Declaration of Independence

Some may have learned the name of his Queen Consort and her accomplishments, but her ethnicity has been ignored (or denied) by most textbooks and historical writers.

Charlotte's depiction as a person of color was unusual for her time. Artists were inclined to soften a subject's features, or in the case of prominent persons of color, to "whitewash" them. Sir Allan Ramsay portrayed Charlotte as distinctively "mulatto". Ramsey was an outspoken abolitionist, and an uncle, by marriage, of Dido (Elizabeth) Belle Lindsay. Dido was the mulatto daughter of a royal British Navy Captain, Sir John Lindsay, and an African slave, he met in the Caribbean, named Maria Belle. Ramsay's second wife was Margaret Lindsay, the Captain's sister. The Captain sent Dido to his uncle, William Murray, the First Earl of Mansfield, and his wife, who were childless. The Murray's raised both Dido and her first cousin (once removed), Elizabeth Murray.

Figure 3 Dido and Elizabeth

The artist's anti-slavery sentiments and familial connection to Dido, may have influenced his portrayal of Charlotte as she really was. His depiction is supported by Charlotte's contemporary, Baron Christian Frederick von Stockmar. Baron von Stockmar was physician to Charlotte's granddaughter, Alexandrina Victoria (more about her later). In von Stockmar's memoirs, published by his son, he noted that Charlotte was possessed of a "...true mulatto face".

2 ROYAL ANCESTRY

Charlotte's racial identity was debated for decades. Many ignored her obvious facial characteristics and denied any possibility that she was of African descent. Her relationship to Margarita de Castro y Sousa was documented in several royal genealogies, but ethnicity is not typically noted in these sources. The racial identification of Margarita's family was documented as a result of an investigation embarked upon by art scholars and historians. The focus of their investigation was the 15th century Flemish paintings of the Adoration of the Magi. It was determined that living people of color had to have been the models for the artworks. The accuracy of complexions, facial characteristics and bone structure of quadroons, octoroons, etc. defies the notion that it was achieved through imagination. The models for the Magi had to have been observed, in person. That led to a search to identify the models.

The Flemish paintings of the Adoration of the Magi occurred around the same time that Princess Isabella became the third wife of Phillip the Good, Duke of Burgundy (in 1429-1430). Guests at the wedding, that took place in the Netherlands, were Princess Isabella's African/Portuguese cousins, the de Sousas. The investigators uncovered sufficient evidence to conclude, that the de Sousas were the subjects of the paintings.

There are six lines of Queen Charlotte's family tree that trace back to Margarita. The tradition of European royal inbreeding created a very small gene pool; hence the persistent emergence of African physiognomy over generations, as evidenced by Queen Charlotte, William I Count of Hainaut, Queen Philippa, Edward the Black, and King James I, to name a few.

Tracing further into Charlotte's family history professional genealogist, Mario de Valdes y Cocom, of Boston, Massachusetts traced Margarita's de Sousa line back to Madragana Ben Aloandro Gil. She was the mistress of the fifth King of Portugal, Afonso III. In 1999, 63-year-old Duarte Nuno Souso Chichorro Marcao, a genealogist and distant cousin of Madragana, living in Lisbon, confirmed Valdes y Cocom's research.

Madragana met the Christian king, Afonso III, in 1249 when he conquered Faro, the capital city of the Algarve, in Portugal. Aloandro Ben Bekar (Gil), was the *Alcalde* (Governor) of Faro, and Madragana's father. The surname "Gil" was appended after Madragana and her father (both of Sephardic Jewish heritage), were baptized into the Christian faith (probably to avoid religious persecution). On the occasion of her baptism, Margarita's aged lover,

Afonso III, became her godfather.

Afonso and Madragana had one son, Martin Afonso de Sousa Chicorro. He married into Portuguese royalty, and the trend of inbreeding led to Madragana becoming the ancestor of almost all European royal houses.

More recent African/European marital connections include the 1916 union of Nadejda Mikhailovna de Torby, a great-granddaughter of the African/Russian poet, Alexander Pushkin and British royal, Lord George Mountbatten.

3 INTERESTS and PATRONAGE

Charlotte and George were both passionate about art and music. An accomplished singer, Charlotte was a student of Johann Christian Bach, son of Johann Sebastian Bach. Her voice was described as "very pleasing". Artists and musicians often performed for, and were supported by, the royal couple.

Charlotte was especially generous to 8-year-old Wolfgang Amadeus Mozart and his family, when they visited England, in 1764. They were received at court; and during their first visit, the prodigy, Wolfgang, took a seat at the organ and proceeded to accompany Charlotte as she performed an aria. The following year, Wolfgang's father, Leopold Mozart, published "Opus 3", six sonatas that young Wolfgang composed and dedicated to Queen Charlotte.

Her charitable and philanthropic projects abound. She was founded the Queen Charlotte Maternity Hospital and generously supported The Royal Hospital of St. Katherine, in London. It is now the Royal College of St. Katherine, dedicated to religious and social work.

Charlotte was also keenly interested in botany. At her residence at Kew Palace, she worked with professional botanists, and delighted in the development and design of the grounds. The beautiful Kew Gardens continues to be a major attraction.

Figure 4 Kew Palace and Gardens (photo)

The arts and philanthropy were not her only cares. More serious concerns arose when King George, was confined with what was then believed to be mental illness. The last twenty years of his life were spent in and out of confinement. Their son, George, ruled in his father's stead, and Charlotte was appointed his Regent. Modern scientists have deduced from the recorded symptoms that the King's disease was probably Porphyria, a rare disorder passed down through families, in which an important part of hemoglobin, called heme, is not made properly.

4 ROYAL DESCENDANTS

Queen Charlotte gave birth to fifteen children, nine girls and six boys. Two sons, Alfred and Octavius, died before they were five years old. Thirteen survived to adulthood.

King George's "Royals Marriage Act" was enacted in 1772. Among its several restrictions, no royal under twenty-five years of age could engage in a valid marriage, neither could a valid royal marriage take place without his approval. Marriages in violation of this Act were deemed invalid, and any off-spring were ineligible to accede to the throne. Several of his children married in contravention of the Act, and some others simply cohabitated.

The fourth son of George and Charlotte, Edward Duke of Kent Hanover, married Victoria Maria Louisa of Saxe-Coburg, sister of King Leopold of the Belgians. Edward was over twenty-five and his request for approval was granted by the king. Their only child, Alexandrina Victoria, was George and Charlotte's only legitimate grandchild. Edward predeceased his father and was never king.

When George III died, the crown passed to Edward's brother, George IV. He reigned from 1820 to 1830. George IV was succeeded by William IV, who reigned from 1830 to 1837, and died childless. His niece (Edward's daughter), Alexandrina Victoria, was next in line and became Queen Victoria. To date, she is the longest reigning British monarch (1837 -1901).

Figure 5 Queen Victoria

Queen Victoria married her first cousin (Francis) Albert Augustus Charles Emmanuel of Saxe-Coburg-Gotha, son of her maternal uncle, Duke Ernest I of Saxe-Coburg-Saalfeld.

Nine children were born to Queen Victoria and her Prince Consort. Their princess daughters married into other royal European families. Their African ancestry and the mutant gene for hemophilia that they bore, were passed on to generations of royals on the European continent.

Their first daughter, Victoria, became the spouse of Frederick III of Germany and mother of Kaiser Wilhelm. Alice married the Duke of Hesse; Helena married Prince Kristian of Schleswig-Holstein; Louise married the Marquise of Lorne; and Beatrice's spouse was Prince Henry of Battenburg. The son of Beatrice and Henry became King Edward VII Wettin when he succeeded Victoria and reigned from 1901 to 1910.

George V Windsor succeeded his father, Edward VII, and ruled from 1910 to 1936. During his reign, the family surname Wettin was changed to Windsor. (World War I and British antipathy to anything German prompted the name change.)

George V's first-born son, Edward Duke of Windsor, reigned briefly as King Edward VIII Windsor. He acceded to the throne in January 1937 and abdicated the following December.

His brother, George VI Windsor reigned from 1937 to 1952. George VI, died on 6 Feb 1952, and his daughter, Alexandra Mary Windsor, the great-great-great-great-granddaughter of Queen Charlotte, became Queen Elizabeth II Windsor.

Elizabeth married Philip of Mountbatten, who is also a great-great-great-great-grandchild of Queen Charlotte. Elizabeth and Philip share great-great-grandparents (Victoria and Albert), and are therefore, third cousins.

Figure 6 Queen Elizabeth II

At her coronation, Elizabeth II delivered her "defense of the crown" speech and stated, "…There is also this. I have behind me not only the splendid traditions and the annals of more than a thousand years but the living strength and majesty of the Commonwealth and Empire; of societies old and new; of lands and races different in history and origins but all, by God's Will, united in spirit and in aim."

By the dawn of the 20th century, nearly 150 of Charlotte's grand, great-grand, and great-great-grand children were royals in European countries from Spain to Scandinavia.

5 NAMESAKES

Charlotte's namesakes include Charlotte (the "Queen City") North Carolina; Mecklenburg counties in both North Carolina and Virginia; Charlotte Street and Queen Street in Norfolk County, North Carolina; and in St. John, New Brunswick, Nova Scotia, the street name Studholme was changed to Charlotte Street.

From 1990 until 2013, a statue of Queen Charlotte, by sculptor Raymond Kaskey, was ensconced at Charlotte/Douglas International Airport. (Sadly, artistic license has robbed the queen of her ethnic semblance.)

Figure 7 Statue of Queen Charlotte (photo)

Her unusual forward leaning posture is to give the effect of her being lifted by the wind, as airplanes are so lifted. In her right hand, she holds her royal crown aloft.

In January 2013, her statue was moved from a prominent position opposite the terminal building, to a courtyard between two parking decks, in order to make room for expansion of the airport. As of January 2014, there has been no decision as to the final placement of the statue.

A British ship named for the queen fought in the Battle of Lake Erie, during the War of 1812. The British Captain Robert H. Barclay commanded a fleet of six vessels: the flagship "Detroit"; ship "Queen Charlotte"; brig "Hunter"; two schooners, "Lady Prevost" and "Chappeway"; and sloop "Little Belt". The British fleet was defeated by Commodore Oliver Hazard Perry's American Navy of 532 men, upward of twenty per cent of which were African Americans.

Perry's flagship, the "Lawrence", was named for Captain James Lawrence who died 4 June 1813, prior to the United States' official declaration of war with England. Captain Lawrence's famous final command was: "Don't give up the ship, boys. Burn her!" Commodore Perry's personal flag bore the first five words of the Lawrence quote.

The Queen Charlotte was captured by the Americans on September 10, 1813, and her ensign and pendant (flags) were turned over to Commodore Perry. Her flags, and those of the five other British vessels in Barclay's fleet, are currently in custody of the US Naval Academy at Annapolis, Maryland.

The flower, Bird of Paradise was discovered in South Africa, in 1773. Its botanical name is "Strelitzia Reginae", in her honor.

Figure 8 Strelitzia Reginae

An English treat, "Apple Charlotte", was another namesake. Puréed apples, baked in a dish lined with buttered bread, was a marvelous way to use up bread left over from tea-time. The French patissier, Caramé, replaced the bread with ladyfingers and the apples with Bavarian cream, and since Russian dishes were popular at the time, he called it Charlotte Russe.

As late as the 1950's, peddlers sold Charlotte Russe from glass enclosed push carts, on street corners in Brooklyn, New York. Yellow cake, whipped cream, with a cherry on top, packaged in a paper cup; it was dubbed the "Brooklyn Treat".

Figure 9 Charlotte Russe

The following poem, whose author's name is lost to history, was dedicated to Queen Charlotte on the day of her wedding and subsequent coronation:

> *"Descended from the warlike Vandal race,*
> *She still preserves that title in her face.*
> *Tho' shone their triumphs o'er Numidia's plain,*
> *And Andalusian fields their name retain;*
> *They but subdued the southern world with arms,*
> *She conquers still with her triumphant charms,*
> *O! Born for rule, to whose victorious brow*
> *The greatest monarch of the north must bow"*.

SOURCES

Altoff, Gerard T., *Deep Water Sailor-Shallow Water Soldiers*. Put-in-Bay, Ohio: 1999

Hedley, Olwen, *Queen Charlotte*, London: 1975

Rogers, J.A., *Nature Knows No Color Line*, 3rd.ed.., St. Petersburg, FL: 1980

Sweet Frank W., *Legal History of the Color Line*, Palm Coast FL: 2005

Valdes y Cocom, Mario de, www.pbs.org/wgbb/pages/frontline/shows/secret/famous/royalfamily.htm

Printed in Great Britain
by Amazon